Thoughtless State

Table of contents:
1] Introduction.--------------------------------4

2] Why we should practice thoughtless state.
  A] benefits achieved by practicing thoughtless state.--5
  B] what other options do we have.--------9

3] How to be in thoughtless state.
  A] ways to achieve thoughtless state.----10
  B] advantages and disadvantages of these methods.-------------------------------12

4] How to have ideal weight with thoughtless state.
  A] what are the ways to lose weight------13
  B] How we could apply thoughtless state principles to achieve ideal weight.---------14

5] How to have good health with thoughtless state.
  A] what are the ways to have good health-16
  B] How we could apply thoughtless state principles to achieve good health.----------17

6] How to have financial freedom with thoughtless state.
  A] what are the ways to achieve financial Freedom.---18
  B] How to apply thoughtless state principles to achieve financial freedom----------------------------19

7] How to have good relationship with thoughtless state.
  A] what are the ways to have good relationship-21
  B] How to apply thoughtless state principles to have good relationship.----------------------------22

8] How to have peace of mind with thoughtless state.
  A] what are the ways to have peace of mind.---24
  B] how to apply thoughtless state principles to have peace of mind.-------------------------------25

9] How to be happy with thoughtless state.
  A] what are the ways to be happy .--------------26
  B] how to apply thoughtless state principles to be happy always .-------------------------------------27

10] how to have great social life with thoughtless state.
 A] How to have a great social life.--------29
 B] How to apply thoughtless state principles to have great social life.------------------------31

11] So now you know how to solve all your problems , what next?

A] how to apply this in day to day life.---32
B] what next ?--------------------------------34

1] Introduction:

Thoughtless state is the magic art of solving all problems. Do you know that by thinking no thoughts even for a small amount of time you experience great pleasure which your mind strive for .Not only your mind but all human beings mind want to be in thoughtless state for as long as possible . If this pleasure is given to your mind quite often then it gives you anything you ask from it.

Yes i mean anything, do not take my word for granted practice it for a minute and you will feel immense pleasure . It is used for controlling your mind. And its the only way by which you could understand yourself and the true nature of universe

I bet you on this ask any yogic guru or highly spiritually aligned person and they will tell you the secret behind thoughtless state. Its the place where all miracles happen.

Even if you do not purchase the book I insist you to practice being in the thoughtless state for few minutes . Although by purchasing the book there will be a drastic change in your life.

2] why should we practice thoughtless state?

First let us look at the benefits of thoughtless state:
A] Benefits :

1] It enhances your decision making skills:
Everyday we have to make n number of decisions .And instead of spending so much time in thinking on what to do and what not to do .
What if we could make decisions instantly .
That too most of them or 90% of them will be right . And even with all analytic thinking we can not achieve this success rate of above 90%.
This saves time, and you will have more time to do things which you love to do.

2] you will feel younger :

Most of us will feel stress free after being in thoughtless state and will have increased efficiency in work . This will make us feel good and feel younger.

3] You will be more active:

After being in thoughtless state you will have more clarity in life and this will make you more active .As you will spend less time in doing things which are not important to you and will be having more time to do things which are important to you.

Instead of being in the confused mindset you will have a clear mind. Thats where magic happens and things get to happen for all of us.

4] You will not over think:

Most of us have too much to think about and too little to do. This happens because we think that, by just thinking alone we can achieve our goals and could reach our destiny . But the reality is that just by thinking ,we rarely can get to our destiny . it requires hard work and smart work .
And by being in thoughtless state we will be self aware and can understand how much to think and when to think and when to stop thinking and start taking action.

5] You recognize inspired action:

This is the most important benefit of being in thoughtless state, you get inspired action more often as your mind is clear and most importantly you can recognize it and this is something very powerful which could change your life forever . Just focus on being in thoughtless state you recognize the inspired action . Act on it and you get success its that simple . Its also called by names like intuition, gut feeling.But believe me friends this is the strongest source of energy which could change human life completely.

Inspired action predicts the shortest route between where we are and where we want to be. Most people know it via small voice from within , but you could know it via images ,sounds, insights from nature around you.

I have written 8 books before , but none of them were a big success, i was putting in all the effort ,i was doing lot of hard work , but then i got an inner awakening and it directed me to promote my books in a certain way , which changed my life completely and there was a huge increment in my income level.

This is so powerful that when you act upon this intuition it can make wonders for you. Do not avoid it . Its the magic wand for all your problems.

Not only in work you could apply this to any area of your life. It will still give you best action idea which when acted on gives you victory . This is guaranteed there is no other option .

Thats what i like about inspired action , its so powerful that every time it works , there is not even a small chance of losing .

6]work seems like effortless:

You enjoy your work as you are aligned with your true self .You get control of your mind and prioritizing work becomes easy for you and this in turn guide to work more. As now your subconscious is helping you in achieving your work goals.

B] what other options do we have:

We do have many other options to achieve our life goals , and practicing thoughtless state is not the only one . some of them involves lot of hard work ,preparing plans & strategies there is nothing wrong in them, but does it guarantee you success we do not know.

So its better to go with practice of thoughtless state to achieve all our life goals.

So i suggest you to give this method a try, if you do not experience any results , you can get back to old methods.

Only small investment of your time is required to practice it and no monetary investment is required.

3] How to be in thoughtless state.

A] ways to achieve thoughtless state?

You can achieve thoughtless state by the following methods:
1] Self awareness.
2] deep breathing.
3] High concentration
4] Stare at an object for consistent period of time.
5] deep silence

lets focus on each of them in detail:

1] close your eyes , breathe in and out with a count of 4 inhale, 4 hold, 4 exhale.
Become aware of your thoughts . Do not judge them , just be aware of them , and slowly you will realize that you are getting less thoughts with each breathe in and out.
Now you are completely focused , at this moment you will experience thoughtless state for a fraction of second , which rejuvenates your body. This is how you could achieve thoughtless state by being self aware of your thoughts.

2] Breathe deeply after 10 to 12 breathes you will feel sleepy , and at that moment you will realize thoughtless state.

3] focus all your energy on one goal, have just one goal in your mind, and leave every other goal aside , with this high concentration you achieve thoughtless state, as your mind becomes clear when you are focused on a single goal.

4] Do this practice daily it stabilizes your mind. Stare at an object for a consistent period of time like for 2 to 3 minutes in the beginning , then you can gradually increase it to 10 to 15 minutes . This will help you get less thoughts and at some moment in the process you will reach thoughtless state.

5] Practice silence for an hour , initially you can start with 15 minutes of being silent, that means you do not have to speak for 15 minutes, both internally inside your body or externally outside your body .This will help you reach thoughtless state at some moment , it also helps in finding out inspired action.

B] Advantages and disadvantages of these methods:

Advantages :

1] Does not require much time to learn, easy to start and experience.
2] provides benefits every time .
3] instant results for all are obtained irrespective of the skill level .
4] Good for health, wealth, and happiness.
5] This is the future of human creativity . This is where most creative things have evolved and will evolve in the future.

Disadvantages:

1] its easy to do, so most people do not recognize its importance.
2] people start it , but do not continue it , as they feel excited about it , and then stop doing it.
3] even after realizing inspired action, people failed to implement it this leads to loss of faith in this method.

4] How to have ideal weight with thoughtless state.

A] what are the ways to lose weight

There are plenty of ways to lose weight , some of them are listed below:
A] swimming
B] Running.
C] walking.
D] high intensity workout.
E] dieting.
F] slow eating.
H] Intermittent fasting.
I] water weight cutting.

We all have heard and might have practiced one or all of the above ways to lose weight:
 Now just give the thoughtless state a chance for 2 to 3 days and see how lighter you feel.

B] How we could apply thoughtless state principles to achieve ideal weight.

Start with self awareness . Most of us do emotional eating, you will feel that you are full while eating, but you still consume more food . This is because your subconscious is protecting you from losing weight . Have an deep conversation with your subconscious and explain it, that you want to lose weight and it should help you to do so.

Start with closing your eyes , take deep breath, then ask a question internally that why you are not at your ideal weight . What is the reason you have over eating issue, there has to be some deep down fear, like if you reach your ideal weight then people may start teasing you, that may be your fear and this is the reason why your mind stops you from losing weight.

There are ways by which you can lose weight . But your mind is not allowing you to reach that state .we have to figure out first internally then things start to change externally.

This is the main reason why most people do not achieve there ideal weight its because there subconscious have a related fear tied to it and its protecting them from the effects.

They have to have a clear conversation with there mind, and find the fear associated with this . Then they can practice any of the ways mentioned in the above section to reach there ideal weight.

5] How to have good health with thoughtless state.
  A] what are the ways to have good health

There are plenty of ways to always have good health, some of them are mentioned below:

1] Drink warm water most of the time.
2] avoid added sugar as much as possible.
3] early to bed and early to rise makes a man healthy, wealthy and wise. Its true in real life too.
4] Avoid junk food as much as possible.
5] exercise at least 10 minutes a day.
6] take medicines at time if you are prescribed by doctor. Do not skip it and get into trouble .

B] How we could apply thoughtless state principles to achieve good health.

Most people go thorough some form of phobia which keeps them away from good health, as if you practice the above habits you will be healthy , there is no other way out, but if you have some fear engraved in your mind, which keeps you away from good health , then it has to be cleared.

We will start with subconscious clearing . It starts with praying to god, asking him to give you good health, and have complete faith in god that he will give you good health. Its the faith that makes all the difference.

Praying to god is an effective way to solve all our problems.
I am sure that if you just remember the below sentence you will have a great life.

" Those who have complete faith in god , will lack nothing in life".

6] How to have financial freedom with thoughtless state.

A] what are the ways to achieve financial freedom.

Broadly speaking there are four ways from which you could earn money, they are as follows:
1] Investing.
2] Business.
3] Self employed.
4] Job.

You just have to focus on one thing initially then went on to work with other segments, but until you reach a platform, it is suggested that you should just focus on one thing, as in the beginning we think of being jack of all, and try to do many things, but the reality is that we should be master of one.

B] how to apply thoughtless state principles to achieve financial freedom

when you have practiced self awareness, you will recognize your inner voice, which is called as inspired action, and when you act on it consistently , you will gain financial freedom in less than 1 month.

The reason why i am am sure that within one month you will reach financial freedom after you act on inspired action consistently is that , inspired action is the shortest path between where you are to what you want to be in life.

There is no other best path out there, this is the best path. And i insist that always act on your inspired action and not on any other action, as we should not settle for second best.
As our best product is one which will give us victory and will help us to reach financial freedom.

As I always Say. Do not take my word for granted , just act on your inspired action consistently and you will see a sharp increase in your income level.

But remember do not share it with others in the beginning as everyone may not support you in the first place .
There opinion may effect your journey in reaching to financial freedom.

7] How to have good relationship with thoughtless state.
 A] what are the ways to have good relationship

There are plenty of ways to have good relationships , some of them are mentioned below:

1] let go of your ego and save the relationship:
 Always its important that we save the relationship and let go of our ego, as when ego goes everything else comes and when ego comes everything else goes.

2] Read at least 10 minutes a day :
By reading most of the self help books, your mind stabilizes and maintain a positive state , for a consistent period of time. This help you have good relationship with yourself and with others as well.

3] Meditate:
Meditation helps you get clarity of mind.
This helps you in being calm and avoiding fights with your peer members for small things.

4] exercise at least 10 minutes a day:
Exercise helps you feel good, which help you maintain good relationship with yourself and with others around you.

B] How to apply thoughtless state principles to have good relationship.

By practicing self awareness you reach complete peace of mind, which help you to be happy and maintain good relationships.

Start with small meditation ritual in the morning for as little as 5 minutes , and gradually increase it to 1 hour in 1 month time, you will see a drastic improvement in relationship with yourself and with others as well.

8] How to have peace of mind with thoughtless state.

A] what are the ways to have peace of mind.

There are plenty of ways to have peace of mind, some of them are listed below:

1] Read for at-least 10 minutes a day:
 Reading stabilizes your mind and you experience inner peace.

2] Journal your thoughts in a dairy :
 Writing makes you feel light and gives you peace of mind.

3] Practice deep breathing:
 Deep breathing help to silence your mind and gives you peace of mind.

4] Practice silence for 15 minutes at-least:
 Try to not speak for at-least 15 minutes everyday , this single habit will help you clear your mind and will give you peace of mind.

B] how to apply thoughtless state principles to have peace of mind.

Practicing self awareness will give you clarity of mind, and this will help you have peace of mind.

Start with meditation for 5 minutes a day. You will feel great relief and can concentrate more on the things which are important to you.
You can priorities things more clearly and can understand yourself in and out.
This helps you in having peace of mind.

9] How to be happy with thoughtless state.
 A] what are the ways to be happy

There are plenty of ways to be happy always, some of them are listed below:

1] help someone in need.
2] spend some time with a child under 5 years old.
3] Draw or paint.
4] sing, dance or cook, practice any of your hobby with sheer dedication.
5] speak with your loved ones.
6] hangout with your friends.
7] watch comedy movies or talk shows.

B] How to apply thoughtless state principles to be happy always

When you practice self awareness you will realize that most of your thoughts do not make any sense at all. Most of These negative thoughts are just opinion of someone else dumped upon you. So just be aware of them and do not judge them. They make no good to you nor to others or to the society at large.

When you understand the root cause of all these thoughts you will realize that they originate from others opinion of yours and they do not have any fact attached to it.
As someone s believe about you can not be the truth. And the word believe consists of lie in between. So its important to believe but its even more important to believe in good things.

This is the key to be happy .By practice of thoughtless state .
Become self aware of your thoughts and it will certainly make you more happy and help you to be in present.

Another practice is to start living in present. Forget the past and the future . Just focus on the present and you are relieved from all the stress existing in your life.

As whatever you can do in your life has to be done in present only . There is no way you could be existing in past or in future . All other states are either happened or will happen and even it is completely dependent on what is happening.

So never let anything or anyone destroy your inner peace by any reason. As someones opinion about you cannot be true.

10] how to have great social life with thoughtless state.

A] How to have a great social life.

Everyone have a social need and it has to be full filled . Specially people in US and UK are more social than in India .
People follow free culture in western countries .
But even though if you are finding it difficult to be social .
Follow the below given steps and it will help you have a great social life.

1] Make new friends. If your old friends are finding it difficult to speak to you no issues make new friends .

2] Join a community and hang out with like minded people who share same passion as you do. You could spend quality time with them as they will understand you very well.

3] Join a non profit organization. Or if you are working in a corporate then enroll yourself in CSR activity as this will help you have stronger bonds between your peer members and your society at large.

4] Go out with your new friends .If your social life is dull then probably its because your old friends have problems with you. Thats what the case in most peoples life . So let go of friends who do not accept you completely as friendship is all about " A friend in need is a friend in deed"

B] How to apply thoughtless state principles to have great social life.

Practice deep breathing, it cancels your negative thoughts and gives you complete light or purity for some time. Then you will realize that all bad things exists within yourself and do not exist outside of you.

I will tell you another practice which could make wonders for you :

Close your eyes and then imagine a small campfire in front of you. Add all your past memories in it and do it until all your past memories are burnt. And then slowly open your eyes you will feel completely free and will have no bad feelings for anyone.

Practice above exercises when you are having bad thoughts for others. After the practice you will feel completely light and will have only good thoughts.

11] So you now know how to solve all your problems , what next?

A] how to apply this in day to day life.
Below are the ways by which you could insert thoughtless state practice before every activity in your daily routine:

1] As soon as you get up , practice meditation for 5 minutes .
Close your eyes and imagine a campfire in front of you and add all your past memories into it. You will feel lighter and will have high concentration throughout the day.

2] After bath in the morning, pray to god or universal energy for at least 2 minutes . It will help you connect with the source.

3] while having breakfast become self aware of your thoughts this will help you get rid of emotional eating.

4] At work practice silence for first 15 minutes of the start of the work . You will get in aligned with your true self and can concentrate better.

5] After lunch relax for few minutes it will provide rest to your body and then you can concentrate better.

6] At evening when you come back from work . Spend some quality time with your family members .This will make your family bonds stronger.

7] Practice self awareness, focus on one object for a consistent period of time , focus on one goal for next day. All these thoughtless state practices when done 1 hour before sleep will give some work for your subconscious mind during sleep.

B] what next?

Now you know how to solve all your problems with being in thoughtless state . Practice it daily and it will change your life drastically .

As i always say do not take my word for granted practice thoughtless state for few days and you will see drastic change in your life for sure.

Thanks
With regards
Sunil Jain

www.ingramcontent.com/pod-product-compliance
Lightning Source LLC
Chambersburg PA
CBHW030739180526
45157CB00008BA/3246